WHAT'S WRONG
IN THE
CITY?

ILLUSTRATED BY JOHN HOLLADAY

There are five things wrong
in each colorful scene.
Can you find them all?

SMITHMARK

NEW YORK

SEATTLE

ANSWERS

There are five things wrong in each scene.

ATLANTA
(1) zebra on sidewalk; (2) one section of railing has vertical bars instead of horizontal; (3) soda bottle on top of building; (4) red car is upside-down; (5) red car is missing a wheel.

BOSTON
(1) ice-cream soda on top of lamppost; (2) on church, one window on the bottom row has a different pattern; (3) life preserver around clock on church; (4) jack-in-the-box on top of building; (5) pink tree.

CHICAGO
(1) missing flagpole; (2) fish in windows of building; (3) traffic signal has green light on top, red light on bottom; (4) red car has no driver; (5) dog is driving taxi.

LOS ANGELES
(1) woman wearing red high heels; (2) man wearing business suit; (3) sign says "BEACH CLOSED"; (4) woman wearing white sock on one foot; (5) man riding skateboard in water.